Windows 10 at the command-line

Quick reference guide to Windows 10's command-line

Part II

About the author

RICCARDO RUGGIU was born in Cagliari in 1976.
He has been working in the silicon-based technology sector for over twenty years, and has gained solid experience working for the most important IT companies in Italy and abroad.
Music has a great impact in his spare time; he is an expert musician (piano, synth and guitar), Dj and deep connoisseur of home and professional audio equipment.

Acknowledgements

Special thanks to my family, and friends, for having always been present.

This book is dedicated to all the curious, those who never tire of learning and are always looking for alternative and better solutions... to become better technicians!

R.Ruggiu

Limit of Liability/Disclaimer of Warranty

Introduction

Here we are, at the second part of this quick guide about the command-line.

Microsoft has never thought of dismissing the command-line, and now that you already know how to juggle the commands learned in the previous book, I can reveal you that with Windows 10 has been also implemented copy/paste with the CTRL + C and CTRL + V keys (you can enable the functionality by clicking on properties and check the options tab).

This second part "definitely raises the bar" and takes into consideration a whole series of known and lesser known commands, highlighting the effectiveness and at the same time the danger of some commands (if not used in the correct way); examines some controls that could be useless in their simplicity, but in reality are very effective if used intelligently and above all in the correct context.

If you are a good technician (or could be), you should be able to master the command prompt at best.

Surely this second part, will be useful going on with the journey in the command prompt and helps you in small and large daily computer challenges.

As in the first volume, I have divided this second part into three chapters; the first examines various configurations and utilities.

The second deals with utilities and checks in the context of computer networks.

The third provides useful commands when the PC enters, as we could say "the workshop" to receive the care of the personnel of the technical assistance laboratory; these commands will help you diagnose the problem, recover important information and data for the timely resolution of faults.

I just have to wish you enjoy the reading!

Contents

Chapter I : Various configurations and utilities
Converting FAT partitions to NTFS

Even if today all PCs for sale already have the hard disk formatted in NTFS, you may have to convert a disk (or a USB flash drive for example) to NTFS format.
To proceed with the convertion, you can use the convert utility.
If you want to convert the PC HDD, here is the command to type:

convert C: /fs:ntfs

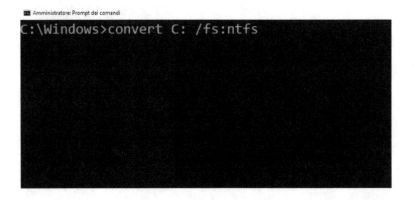

In this case, the option "/fs:ntfs" specify that you want the volume (C:) to be converted to NTFS.

IMPORTANT: if you need to convert the hard disk on

which the operating system is installed, the operation will be carried out when the PC is restarted, since the hard disk is blocked by the operating system itself.

In case you want to convert a USB flash drive, you just have to change the letter of the corresponding volume (es. D, E, etc.).

Below is the list of other available options:

/V   Specifies that the conversion will be executed in verbose mode.
/CvtArea:filename
            Specifies a contiguous file in the root directory that will be used as a place holder for NTFS system files.
/NoSecurity Specifies that the security settings in the converted directories and files will allow access to all users.
/X   Forces the volume to dismount before proceeding with the conversion.
            The system close all handles, and all the open files will become inaccessible.

2

Updating group policy with GPUpdate utility

The GPUpdate utility (Group Policy Update), allows you to update group policies on a PC within a domain.

This utility is very useful if you want to try to fix issues on PCs that are always on 24 hours a day; in this way you can update the computer with the latest group policies, if new ones have been implemented.

It replaces the /refreshpolicy option of the SecEdit utility, which has been discontinued and therefore can no longer be used.

The command output is shown below:

```
C:\Users\    rrug    >gpupdate /force
Updating policy...

Computer Policy update has completed successfully.
User Policy update has completed successfully.


C:\Users\    rrug    >
```

The /force option in the GPUpdate utility, re-applies all policy settings.
By default, are updated only the changed policy settings.

Compact utility

One characteristic of the NT file system (or NTFS) is the option that allows to compress files.

This feature offers two advantages; the first one, is the ability to store a bigger amount of data on a single hard drive.

The second, is a slight performance boost by compressing files (if compared to the same amount of files not compressed).

Unlike other commands/utilities, Compact, doesn't displays an output in the form of a table; each line displays a sequence of items used to determine the compression ratio:

```
C:\>COMPACT

Elenco C:\
I nuovi file aggiunti a questa directory non verranno compressi.

        0 :          0 = 1,0 a 1    $WINRE_BACKUP_PARTITION.MARKER
        1 :          1 = 1,0 a 1    BOOTNXT
       80 :         80 = 1,0 a 1    bootTel.dat
```

The bottom of the command output, shows a summary of the directory information, including the number of the compressed and uncompressed files, the current size and the compression ratio:

```
Amministratore: Riccardo Ruggiu                                    —  □  ×
Dei 37 file nelle 1 directory
0 sono compressi e 37 sono non compressi.
9.731.441.459 byte complessivi di dati memorizzati in 9.731.441.459 byte.
Il rapporto di compressione è 1,0 a 1.
```

The list below describes each of the commands:

/C   Compresses the specified files. Directories will be marked in order that all the files added later on will be compressed, unless /EXE is specified.

/U   Uncompresses the specified files. Directories will be marked in order that all the files added later on are not compressed.

If **/EXE** is specified, only files that are compressed as executable will be decompressed. If the argument is omitted, only NTFS compressed files will be decompressed.

/S   Performs the specified task on the files of the specified directory and all subdirectories.

The default directory is the current one.

/A   Shows files with hidden or system attributes. The default is that these files are omitted.

/I   Continue to perform the specified operation even after errors have occurred.
The default setting provides that Compact stops when meets an error.

/F   Forces the compression operation on all specified files, even those that are already compressed.
By default, files that have already been compressed are skipped.

/Q   Reports only essential information.

/EXE Use optimized compression for frequently read, unmodified executable files.
The supported algorithms are:
      XPRESS4K (the fastest) (default)
      XPRESS8K
      XPRESS16K
      LZX   (higher compression)

/CompactOs Set or query the compression status of the system. The supported options are:

query - Query the compact status of the system.

always – Compress all binary files of the operating system and set the system state as compact, kept until changed by the administrator.

never - Unzips all operating systems binary files and set the system state as non-compact, which is retained until changed by the administrator.

/WinDir Used with /CompactOs:query, when querying the offline operating system.
Specifies the directory where Windows is installed.

fileame Specififies a search criterion, file or directory.

Used without parameters, COMPACT shows the compression status of the current directory and the files it contains.
Multiple filenames and wildcard characters can be used.
You need to insert spaces between multiple parameters.

Compressing files

Many people think that to compress a file or create compressed file archives it's necessary to have third party software (WinZip and/or WinRAR just to quote a couple of the most famous).
You can use the "cabinet" file format provided by Windows (cab).
If you try to do a search on your pc, you'll find that there are a lot of CAB files.
In fact, Microsoft usually compresses many application files related to Windows setup.

MakeCAB is the tool that Windows gives to compress files.

The utility uses the following syntax:

MAKECAB [/V[n]] [/D var=value ...] [/L dir] source [destination]
MAKECAB [/V[n]] [/D var=value ...] /F directive_file [...]

The following list describes each of the commands:

source   File to compress.
destination   File name to give compressed file. If omitted, the last character of the source file name is replaced with an underscore (_) and used as the destination.
/F directives A file with MakeCAB directives (may be repeated). Refer to Microsoft Cabinet SDK for information on directive_file.
/D var=value Defines variable with specified value.
/L dir   Location to place destination (default is current directory).
/V[n]   Verbosity level (1..3).

Sharing folders

You can use the SHRPubW utility for sharing folders.

C:\Windows>SHRPubW

After typing the command and pressing enter, you will see the graphical interface for shared folder wizard as a pop-up:

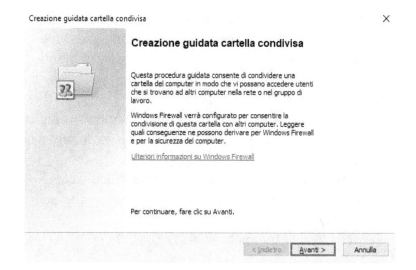

Creazione guidata cartella condivisa   ✕

Creazione guidata cartella condivisa

Questa procedura guidata consente di condividere una cartella del computer in modo che vi possano accedere utenti che si trovano ad altri computer nella rete o nel gruppo di lavoro.

Windows Firewall verrà configurato per consentire la condivisione di questa cartella con altri computer. Leggere quali conseguenze ne possono derivare per Windows Firewall e per la sicurezza del computer.

Ulteriori informazioni su Windows Firewall

Per continuare, fare clic su Avanti.

< Indietro   Avanti >   Annulla

Checking quickly machine's name and user name currently logged into the machine

To quickly check the name of your pc and the name of the user actually logged on, you can use the following command:

C:\Windows>WhoAmI

Here is the output:

In the first part of the output (before the backslash), you can see the name of the pc (desktop-etc.etc.), after the backslash, you can see the user currently logged on the pc (ricky).

Setting and changing the colours of the prompt window

There are two options to change the colors.
You can click in the upper left corner and then on properties as in the figure below:

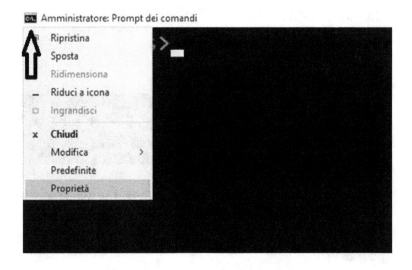

Next, select the "Colors" tab and proceed to change the color of the text and / or the background, such as shown below:

Click ok, to save the changes.

As a second option, you can use the command **color**.

COLOR [attr]

attr   Specifies the color attribute of the console output.

The color attribute consists of TWO hexadecimal digits: the first for the background, the second for the foreground (text) color.
For each of these values it's possible to choose one of the following figures:

0 = Black   8 = Grey
1 = Dark blue   9 = Blu
2 = Green   A = Lemon green
3 = Aqua green   B = Light blue
4 = Bordeaux   C = Red
5 = Purple   D = Fuchsia
6 = Olive green   E = Yellow
7 = Light grey   F = White

So, if you type:

C:\Windows>color 0a

You'll get the black background and the lemon green text color.

And again, color fc sets red as the foreground color and white as the background color.

To restore the default settings, type color and hit enter on your keyboard.

Changing the title of the prompt window

Apparently, it may seem like a pointless thing to you, but changing the title of a window has a reason for being.
For example, if you are monitoring the performances of four devices connected to a network (and consequently you have four windows open), it will be useful to name each window with the name of the device it is monitoring.

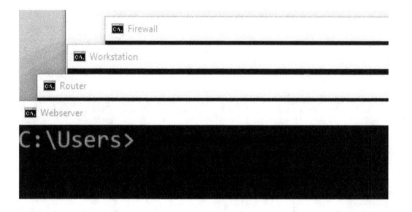

To change the title of a window, you use the title command.

Ex.
C:\Windows>title Firewall

Windows will assign different processes to each open window:

File   Opzioni   Visualizza

Processi   Prestazioni   Cronologia applicazioni   Avvio   Utenti   Dettagli   Servizi

Nome	Stato	83% CPU	86% Memoria
⌄ Processore dei comandi di Windows (2)		0%	6,2 MB
Firewall		0%	0,6 MB
Host finestra console		0%	5,6 MB
⌄ Processore dei comandi di Windows (2)		0%	6,5 MB
Host finestra console		0%	5,8 MB
Webserver		0%	0,6 MB
⌄ Processore dei comandi di Windows (3)		0,7%	6,9 MB
Comando Ping TCP/IP		0,7%	0,5 MB
Host finestra console		0%	5,6 MB
Workstation - ping 127.0.0.1 -t		0%	0,8 MB
⌄ Processore dei comandi di Windows (2)		0%	6,4 MB
Host finestra console		0%	5,7 MB
Router		0%	0,6 MB

Furthermore, Windows will associate the settings changes with the title of the window from which the command was started.

18

On screen keyboard

Using the on-screen keyboard can be very useful in terms of security and privacy.

For example, if you have to type your credit card information or other important data on a PC that aren't using only you and prefer not incur any risk with unpleasant surprises, the on-screen keyboard is for you.

The company you work for, may have installed without your knowledge a "Keylogger" (software / hardware that is able to detect and store everything that is typed on the keyboard) on the company PC, or a virus may have installed one on your personal pc without your knowledge, communicating your data to some offender.

Typing the command osk (On Screen Keyboard) and pressing enter on the keyboard,

a keyboard will appear (as a popup) on the screen as in the example below:

To write, you'll need to use the mouse.

IMPORTANT: when using the on-screen keyboard, be careful that there is no one behind you reading what you're typing (shoulder surfing), particularly if you are in the office or in a public place.

The runas command

If you're working on a PC connected to a domain, and/or on which multiple users with different privileges are configured, the **runas** command can be very useful.

Imagine being logged into the PC as a "normal" user and therefore not having the rights to install and/or use a software.

You should log out and log back in with a user with administrator privileges.

Otherwise, you can do the same using the runas command.

If you want to run the registry as an administrator you'll have to type as follows:

runas /user:administrator regedit

After pressing enter, the system will ask for the password:

```
C:\Windows>runas /user:administrator regedit
Immettere la password per administrator:
```

In the example shown, "administrator" is the user configured on the PC with administrator privileges. Logically, you'll need to indicate the correct user based on the configuration of your pc/domain.

To run command prompt as administrator, type as below:

runas /user:administrator cmd

Same thing if you want to start any program, you'll have to write as below:

runas   /user: domain_name\administrator_account program name

To run a batch file (.bat), type as in the example:

runas /user:administrator C:\data\batchfile.bat

In addition to the administrator user, you'll also need to indicate the path to the .bat file.

In all cases, after clicking on enter, the system will ask you to enter the administrator password.

Comparing the contents of two files or groups of files

The **comp** utility allows you to compare two or more files. It's often used on text files, to verify that there are no differences between the two files, or to find duplicate files.

Below is the syntax of the command:

COMP [data1] [data2] [/D] [/A] [/L] [/N=number] [/C] [/OFF[LINE]] [/M]

   data1   Specifies the position and the name of the source file for the comparison.
   data2   Specifies the position and the name of the destination file for the comparison.
/D   Displays the differences in decimal format.
/A   Displays the differences in ASCII characters.
/L   Displays the line numbers for differences.
/N=number Compares only the specified number of lines in each file.
   /C   Ignore case difference of ASCII characters when comparing files.
   /OFF[LINE] It doesn't ignore files where the offline attribute is set.
   /M   It doesn't require you to compare multiple files.

Viewing and managing services

When issues occur, it's useful to check the active services on the PC.
It's also possible to check them via the command line.
To get the list of active services on the machine, you can type the command ***net start***.

Below is the output:

```
Amministratore Prompt dei comandi                                          –  □  ×

C:\Windows>net start
I seguenti servizi di Windows sono avviati:

    Accesso dati utente_7c260
    Acquisizione di immagini di Windows (WIA)
    Adobe Acrobat Update Service
    Agent Activation Runtime_7c260
    Agente mapping endpoint RPC
    Aggiorna il servizio Orchestrator
    Alimentazione
    Archiviazione dati utente_7c260
    Assistente per l'accesso all'account Microsoft
    Audio di Windows
    BFE (Base Filtering Engine)
    Cache tipi di carattere Windows Presentation Foundation 3.0.0.0
    Centro sicurezza PC
```

Let's assume the scenario in which the user has launched prints but everything has stopped.

One of the things to check is that the "Print Spooler" (the service that manages the printing process on the PC) is active.

To check it, you'll need to check that it's present in the list of the output generated by the command on the previous page.

Well, you've checked and it's active... however sometimes it's useful to restart the service.

In this case, you'll need to stop it with the **net stop** command followed by the name of the service you want to stop.

Below is the output:

```
Amministratore: Prompt dei comandi

C:\Windows>net stop spooler
Il servizio Spooler di stampa sta per essere arrestato.
Servizio Spooler di stampa arrestato.
```

To start the service, type the *net start* command followed by the name of the service you want to start.

Below is the output:

```
Amministratore: Prompt dei comandi

C:\Windows>net start spooler
Servizio Spooler di stampa in fase di avvio .
Avvio del servizio Spooler di stampa riuscito.
```

At this point, if the issue is related to the print spooler service, the printer will start to activate and produce the required printouts.

Redirecting the output of a command to the Windows clipboard

To redirect the output to the Windows clipboard, you can use the *clip* utility.
This utility must be "queued" by "piping" to the command whose output you want to save.

Below is an example:

```
Amministratore: Prompt dei comandi

C:\Windows>dir | clip

C:\Windows>ping 127.0.0.1 | clip

C:\Windows>
```

Chapter II   Networking: configurations and checks
Mapping a network drive and connecting to shared resources

To map a network drive, you can use the *net use* command.
Choose a letter for the drive (ex.Y) or type an asterisk (*) instead of indicating a letter and the system will automatically assign a letter starting from Z and going back in alphabetical order, until it finds the first available letter.

Here is an example:

net use Y: \\computername\sharename

You can also connect to a shared resource on another PC by typing the command:

net use \\computername\sharename

To see shared resources in real time, type net use.
For more options, type net use /? in the command prompt.

Sharing resources on the network with other users and/or computers

You can view, create, modify and delete shared resources as with the graphical interface.

For example, you can share a folder or hard disk with other users connected on the same network.

To see the list of shared resources, you can type *net share*:

```
C:\Windows>net share

Nome cond.    Risorsa                      Nota
-----------------------------------------------------------------

C$            C:\                          Condivisione predefinita

G$            G:\                          Condivisione predefinita

IPC$                                       IPC remoto

ADMIN$        C:\WINDOWS                   Amministrazione remota

Esecuzione comando riuscita.
```

This command uses the following syntax:

Command syntax:

NET SHARE sharename
                sharename=drive:path
                [/GRANT:user,[READ | CHANGE | FULL]]

```
         [/USERS:number | /UNLIMITED]
         [/REMARK:"text"]
             [/CACHE:Manual | Documents| Programs
| BranchCache | None ]
       sharename    [/USERS:number    |    /UNLIMITED]
[/REMARK:"text"]
                          [/CACHE:Manual | Documents
| Programs | BranchCache | None]
       {sharename | devicename | drive:path} /DELETE
       sharename \\computername /DELETE
```

The following list *describes the purpose of each command;*

drive:path　　　specifies the path of the drive. Must contain the drive letter, the colon and the right path.

/USERS:number　　defines the maximum number of users who can access at the same time the shared resource.

/UNLIMITED　　specifies that an unlimited number of users can access at the same time to the shared resource.

/REMARK:"text"   Provides a descriptive comment on the share resource. It's important to insert an optimal description between the quotation marks, so that the users can easily find the resource.

devicename   Defines one or more printers (from port LPT1: up to LPT9:) through the sharename.

/DELETE   Stops the sharing of a resource.

For more details you can type *net help share* and press enter.

Disabling and enabling the Wi-Fi interface (or the Ethernet one)

It may happen that the wireless interface of a laptop (for example) stops working properly.
It's possible to disable and re-enable it via the command prompt to restore proper operation.
After starting the prompt as administrator, enter the netsh context and type the command:

interface set interface "Wi-fi" disable

Check to see if the wireless interface has been properly disabled:

```
netsh>interface set interface "Wi-fi" disable

netsh>interface show interface

Stato admin     Stato          Tipo          Nome interfaccia
------------------------------------------------------------------
Abilitato       Disconnesso    Dedicato      Ethernet 2
Abilitato       Disconnesso    Dedicato      Ethernet 3
Disabilitato    Disconnesso    Dedicato      Wi-Fi
Abilitato       Disconnesso    Dedicato      Ethernet

netsh>
```

Proceed now to re-enable the interface with the command:

interface set interface "Wi-fi" enable

Check to see if the wireless interface has been properly re-enabled:

Now the Wi-Fi interface has been re-enabled and it's again possible to navigate correctly.

Note: the sequence of commands indicated is also valid for the Ethernet interface; just change the command, replacing "Wi-Fi" with "Ethernet".

Resetting TCP/IP's stack to default settings

If you've carried out all the necessary checks and want to reset the TCP/IP settings of your PC, you can type the following command *int ip reset reset.log command*, from the netsh context; below is the output:

netsh>int ip reset reset.log command
Reimpostazione di Inoltro raggruppamento completata.
Reimpostazione di Raggruppamento completata.
Reimpostazione di Protocollo di controllo completata.
Reimpostazione di Richiesta sequenza echo completata.
Reimpostazione di Globale completata.
Reimpostazione di Interfaccia completata.
Reimpostazione di Indirizzo Anycast completata.
Reimpostazione di Indirizzo multicast completata.
Reimpostazione di Indirizzo Unicast completata.
Reimpostazione di Router adiacente completata.
Reimpostazione di Percorso completata.
Reimpostazione di Potenziale completata.
Reimpostazione di Criteri di prefisso completata.
Reimpostazione di Router adiacente proxy completata.
Reimpostazione di Route completata.

Reimpostazione di Prefisso del sito completata.
Reimpostazione di Sottointerfaccia completata.
Reimpostazione di Pattern di attivazione completata.
Reimpostazione di Risolvi router adiacente completata.
Reimpostazione di completata.
Reimpostazione di completata.
Reimpostazione di completata.
Reimpostazione di completata.
Reimpostazione di non riuscita.
Accesso negato.
Reimpostazione di completata.
Reimpostazione di completata.
Reimpostazione di completata.
Reimpostazione di completata.
Reimpostazione di completata.
Reimpostazione di completata.
Reimpostazione di completata.
Riavviare il computer per completare l'azione.

netsh>

Windows Firewall: show state, show config

You can retrieve the Windows firewall configuration and status information via the netsh context.

Type the command: ***netsh firewall show state***

```
■ Amministratore: Prompt dei comandi                                    -  □  X
C:\WINDOWS\system32>netsh firewall show state

Stato firewall:
-------------------------------------------------------------------
Profilo                                 = Standard
Modalità operativa                      = Attiva
Modalità eccezioni                      = Attiva
Modalità risposta multicast/broadcast   = Attiva
Modalità notifiche                      = Attiva
Versione criterio di gruppo             = Windows Defender Firewall
Modalità amministrazione remota         = Disattiva

Porte attualmente aperte su tutte le interfacce di rete:
Porta  Prot.    Versione Programma
-------------------------------------------------------------------
Nessuna porta attualmente aperta su tutte le interfacce di rete.
IMPORTANTE: comando eseguito.
"netsh firewall" è tuttavia deprecato.
Utilizzare invece "netsh advfirewall firewall".
Per ulteriori informazioni sull'utilizzo dei comandi "netsh advfirewall fir
```

Although the output indicates that this is a "deprecated" command (used in the past as official documentation, but whose use is currently discouraged in favor of the newer "netsh advfirewall firewall" version), it provides a fairly complete overview of the status of the firewall and is simpler and more immediate to use than its successor.

To check the configuration, type the following command:
netsh firewall show config

```
Amministratore: Prompt dei comandi                              -  □  ×
C:\WINDOWS\system32>netsh firewall show config

Configurazione profilo Dominio:
-------------------------------------------------------------
Modalità operativa                      = Attiva
Modalità eccezioni                      = Attiva
Modalità di risposta multicast/broadcast = Attiva
Modalità notifiche                      = Attiva

IMPORTANTE: "netsh firewall" è deprecato.
Utilizzare "netsh advfirewall firewall".
Per ulteriori informazioni sull'utilizzo dei comandi "netsh advfirewall fir
ewall"
invece di "netsh firewall", vedere l'articolo della Knowledge Base 947709
all'indirizzo https://go.microsoft.com/fwlink/?linkid=121488 .


C:\WINDOWS\system32>
```

Again, we're reminded that the command is "deprecated", and Windows recommends the use of "netsh adv firewall firewall".

IMPORTANT: in case you've tried all the troubleshooting to fix a network issue, but without success, you can try to disable the firewall as a last resort (you shouldn't disable the firewall as an attempt to fix an issue, unless it's strictly necessary).

By disabling the firewall, you notice if the issue occurs when the firewall is active.

If disabling the firewall you notice that a certain application is working properly, it will be useful to check the site of the manufacturer of the app that isn't working well and check if an update is available that allows the application to work properly, even with the firewall active.

Other commands for collecting data and Windows Firewall configuration

Still within the netsh context, there are other commands available;

show allowedprogram   (shows the allowed programs).

Below is the output:

netsh firewall>show allowedprogram

Configurazione programmi consentiti per il profilo Dominio:
Modalità   Direzione traffico   Nome/Programma

Configurazione programmi consentiti per il profilo Standard:
Modalità   Direzione traffico   Nome/Programma

Attiva   In entrata   D-Link Click'n Connect / D:\d-link.exe

Attiva   In entrata   Firefox (C:\Program Files\Mozilla Firefox) / C:\Program Files\Mozilla Firefox\firefox.exe

Attiva   In entrata   exe / C:\program files (x86)\hd-ip01 cam view\camview.exe

show config   (shows detailed information about the local configuration).

below is the output:

netsh firewall>show config

Configurazione profilo Dominio:

Modalità operativa   = Attiva
Modalità eccezioni   = Attiva
Modalità di risposta multicast/broadcast = Attiva
Modalità notifiche   = Attiva

show portopening (shows the firewall port configuration).

Examples:

    show portopening
    show portopening ENABLE
    show portopening verbose=ENABLE

below is the output:

netsh firewall>show portopening

Configurazione porte per il profilo Dominio:
Porta Protocollo Modalità Direzione traffico Nome

Configurazione porte per il profilo Standard:
Porta Protocollo Modalità Direzione traffico Nome
----

show state   (shows current status information).

Below is the output:

netsh firewall>show state

Stato firewall:

Profilo   = Standard
Modalità operativa   = Attiva
Modalità eccezioni   = Attiva
Modalità risposta multicast/broadcast = Attiva
Modalità notifiche   = Attiva
Versione criterio di gruppo   = Windows Defender
Firewall
Modalità amministrazione remota   = Disattiva

Porte attualmente aperte su tutte le interfacce di rete:
Porta Prot.   Versione Programma

Nessuna porta attualmente aperta su tutte le interfacce di rete.

show notifications   (shows the firewall notification
configuration).

below is the output:

netsh firewall>show notifications

Configurazione profilo Dominio:

Modalità notifiche   = Attiva

Configurazione profilo Standard (corrente):

Modalità notifiche   = Attiva

add allowedprogram (adds the configuration of programs allowed by the firewall).

Parameters:

program – Program path and file name.

name – Program name.

mode – Program mode (optional).
    ENABLE - Allow firewall traffic (default).
    DISABLE – Doesn't allow firewall traffic.

scope – scope of the program (optional).
    ALL   - Allows all traffic to pass through the firewall (default).
    SUBNET – Allows only traffic from the local network (subnet).
    CUSTOM – Allows only specified traffic to pass through the firewall.

addresses – Addresses for the custom scope (optional). This comma delimited scope can include IPv4 addresses, IPv6 addresses, subnets, ranges, or the LocalSubnet keyword.

profile – Configuration profile (optional).
CURRENT - For the active profile, that is the domain profile, the standard profile (such as the private profile) or the pubblic profile (default).
DOMAIN - For the domain profile.
STANDARD – For the standard profile, such as the private profile.
ALL - For the domain profile and the standard profile (ex. private), but not for the public one.

Notes: 'addresses' can only be specified if 'scope' is 'CUSTOM'.
The 'addresses' list cannot include unspecified or loopback addresses.

Examples:

add allowedprogram C:\MyApp\MyApp.exe "My Application" ENABLE

add allowedprogram C:\MyApp\MyApp.exe "Applicazione" ENABLE CUSTOM 157.60.0.1,172.16.0.0/16,10.0.0.0/255.0.0.0, 12AB:0000:0000:CD30::/60,LocalSubnet

add allowedprogram program=C:\MyApp\MyApp.exe name="Applicazione" mode=DISABLE

add allowedprogram program=C:\MyApp\MyApp.exe name="Applicazione" mode=ENABLE scope=CUSTOM addresses=157.60.0.1, 172.16.0.0/16,10.0.0.0/255.0.0.0, 12AB:0000:0000:CD30::/60,LocalSubnet

delete allowedprogram (delete the configuration of programs allowed by the firewall).

Parameters:

program – Program path and file name.

profile – Configuration profile (optional).
CURRENT - For the active profile, that is the domain profile, the standard profile (such as the private profile) or the public profile (default).
DOMAIN - For the domain profile.
STANDARD – For the standard profile, such as the private profile.
ALL - For the domain profile and the standard profile (ex. private), but not for the public one.

Examples:

delete allowedprogram C:\MyApp\MyApp.exe
delete allowedprogram program=C:\MyApp\MyApp.exe

set icmpsetting (used to specify the ICMP traffic allowed on the firewall).

Parameters:

type - Type ICMP.
  2   - Allows outbound packets that are too large.
  3   - Allows outbound unreachable destinations.
  4   - Allows slowdown of the output source.
  5   - Allows redirection.
  8   - Allows incoming echo requests.
  9   - Allows incoming router requests.
  11 - Allows the maximum exit time to be exceeded.
  12 - Allows incorrect output parameters.
  13 - Allows incoming timestamp requests.
  17 - Allows incoming mask requests.
  ALL - All types.

mode – ICMP mode (optional).
  ENABLE - Allows firewall traffic   (default).
  DISABLE – Doesn't allow firewall traffic.

profile – Configuration profile (optional).

CURRENT - For the active profile, that is the domain profile, the standard profile (such as the private profile) or the public profile (default).

DOMAIN - For the domain profile.

STANDARD – For the standard profile, such as the private profile.

ALL - For the domain profile and the standard profile (ex. private), but not for the public one.

Examples:

set icmpsetting 8
set icmpsetting 8 ENABLE
set icmpsetting type=ALL mode=DISABLE

set logging (set up tracking on the firewall).

Parameters:

filelocation – Path and file name of the log (optional).

maxfilesize – Maximum size of the log file in kilobytes (optional).

droppedpackets – Log mode of dropped packets (optional).
    ENABLE - Log into the firewall.
    DISABLE – It doesn't log into the firewall.

connections – Successful connection logging mode (optional).
    ENABLE - Log into the firewall.
    DISABLE - It doesn't log into the firewall.

Notes: at least one parameter must be specified.

Examples:

set logging
%systemroot%\system32\LogFiles\Firewall\pfirewall.log
4096 ENABLE
setlogging
filelocation=%systemroot%\system32\LogFiles\Firewall\pf
irewall.log maxfilesize=4096 droppedpackets=ENABLE

set opmode (sets the operational configuration of the firewall both globally and for a specific connection / interface).

Parameters:

mode - Operative mode.
    ENABLE – Enable the firewall.
    DISABLE – Disable the firewall.

exceptions - Exceptions mode (optional).
    ENABLE - Allows traffic through the firewall (default).
    DISABLE - Doesn't allow traffic through the firewall.

profile - Configuration profile (optional)
    CURRENT - For the active profile, that is the domain profile, the standard profile (such as the private profile) or the public profile (default).
    DOMAIN   - For the domain profile.
    STANDARD – For the standard profile, such as the private profile.
    ALL   - For the domain profile and the standard profile (ex. private), but not for the public one.

Examples:

    set opmode ENABLE
    set opmode mode=ENABLE exceptions=DISABLE

add portopening   (used to add the configuration
of a firewall port, TCP or UDP).

add portopening
    [protocol =] TCP|UDP|ALL
    [port =] 1-65535
    [name =] name
    [[mode =] ENABLE|DISABLE
    [scope =] ALL|SUBNET|CUSTOM
    [addresses =] addresses
    [profile =] CURRENT|DOMAIN|STANDARD|ALL

Parameters:

protocol – Protocol for the port.
    TCP - TCP protocol (Transmission Control Protocol).
    UDP - UDP protocol (User Datagram Protocol).
    ALL - All protocols.

port - Port number.

name - Port name.

mode – Port mode (optional).
ENABLE – Allows traffic through the firewall (default).
DISABLE – Doesn't allow traffic through the firewall.

scope – Port scope (optional).
ALL – Allows all traffic to pass through the firewall (default).
SUBNET – Allows only traffic from the local network (subnet).
CUSTOM – Allows only specified traffic to pass through the firewall.

addresses – Addresses for the custom scope (optional).
This comma delimited scope can include IPv4 addresses, IPv6 addresses, subnets, ranges, or the LocalSubnet keyword.

profile – Configuration profile (optional).
CURRENT – For the active profile, that is the domain profile, the standard profile (such as the private profile) or the public profile (default).
DOMAIN – For the domain profile.
STANDARD – For the standard profile, such as the private profile.

ALL – For the domain profile and the standard profile (ex. private), but not for the public one.

Notes: 'addresses' can be only specified if 'scope' is 'CUSTOM'.
    The 'addresses' list cannot include unspecified or loopback addresses.

Examples:

    add portopening TCP 80 "Porta Web"
    add portopening UDP 500 IKE ENABLE ALL
    add portopening ALL 53 DNS ENABLE CUSTOM
        157.60.0.1,172.16.0.0/16,10.0.0.0/255.0.0.0,
        12AB:0000:0000:CD30::/60,LocalSubnet
    add portopening protocol=ALL port=53 name=DNS
mode=ENABLE scope=CUSTOM

addresses=157.60.0.1,172.16.0.0/16,10.0.0.0/255.0.0.0,
    12AB:0000:0000:CD30::/60,LocalSubnet

set portopening   (used to change the TCP or UDP configurations of an existing port on the firewall).

Parameters:

protocol – Protocol for the port.
   TCP – TCP protocol (Transmission Control Protocol).
   UDP – UDP protocol (User Datagram Protocol).
   ALL – All protocols.

port – Port number.

name – Port name (optional).

mode – Port mode (optional).
   ENABLE – Allows traffic through the firewall (default).
   DISABLE – Doesn't allow traffic through the firewall.

   scope – Port scope (optional).
   ALL – Allows all traffic to pass through the firewall (default).

SUBNET – Allows only local network (subnet) traffic to pass through the firewall.

CUSTOM – Allows only specified traffic to pass through the firewall.

addresses – Addresses for the custom scope (optional).
        This comma delimited scope can include IPv4 addresses, IPv6 addresses, subnets, ranges, and the LocalSubnet keyword.

profile - Configuration profile (optional).
        CURRENT - For the active profile, that is the domain profile, the standard profile (such as the private profile) or the public profile (default).
.

        DOMAIN – For the domain profile.
        STANDARD – For the standard profile, such as the private profile.
        ALL – For the domain and standard profile (ex. private), but not for the public one.

Notes: 'addresses' can only be specified if 'scope' is 'CUSTOM'.
        The 'addresses' list cannot include unspecified or loopback addresses.

Examples:

set portopening TCP 80 "Web port"
set portopening UDP 500 IKE ENABLE ALL
set portopening ALL 53 DNS ENABLE CUSTOM
157.60.0.1,172.16.0.0/16,10.0.0.0/255.0.0.0,
12AB:0000:0000:CD30::/60,LocalSubnet
set portopening protocol=ALL port=53 name=DNS
mode=ENABLE scope=CUSTOM

addresses=157.60.0.1,172.16.0.0/16,10.0.0.0/255.0.0.0,
12AB:0000:0000:CD30::/60,LocalSubnet

delete portopening (used to delete the configuration of a firewall TCP or UDP port).

Parameters:

protocol – Protocol for the port
   TCP – TCP protocol (Transmission Control Protocol).
   UDP – UDP protocol (User Datagram Protocol).
   ALL – All protocols.

port - Port number.

profile – Configuration profile (optional).
   CURRENT - For the active profile, that is the domain profile, the standard profile (such as the provate profile) or the public profile (default).
   DOMAIN   - For the domain profile.
   STANDARD - For the standard profile, for example the private profile.
   ALL – For the domain and standard profile (ex. private), but not for the public one.

Examples:

   delete portopening TCP 80
   delete portopening protocol=UDP port=500

set service (used to allow or block RPC and DCOM traffic, file and printer sharing, and UpnP traffic).

Examples:

set service FILEANDPRINT
set service REMOTEADMIN DISABLE
set service REMOTEDESKTOP ENABLE CUSTOM
157.60.0.1,172.16.0.0/16,10.0.0.0/255.0.0.0,
12AB:0000:0000:CD30::/60,LocalSubnet
set service type=UPNP
set service type=REMOTEADMIN mode=ENABLE
scope=SUBNET
set   service   type=REMOTEDESKTOP
mode=ENABLE scope=CUSTOM

addresses=157.60.0.1,172.16.0.0/16,10.0.0.0/255.0.0.0,
12AB:0000:0000:CD30::/60,LocalSubnet

set notifications (used to set user notifications also via popups, when applications try to open enabled ports).

Parameters:

mode - Notification mode.
ENABLE – Allows pop-up notifications from the firewall.
DISABLE – Does not allow pop-up notifications from the firewall.

profile – Configuration profile (optional).
CURRENT - For the active profile, that is the domain profile, the standard profile (such as the provate profile) or the public profile (default).
DOMAIN   - For the domain profile.
STANDARD - For the standard profile, for example the private profile.
ALL – For the domain and standard profile (ex. private), but not for the public one.

Examples:

set notifications ENABLE
set notifications mode=DISABLE

Reset (reset all firewall configuration to default values).

Chapter III Tests/diagnostics and information retrieval
Checking the battery efficiency of a laptop

Many associate the power settings with the time it takes for the monitor to go into stand-by, when the PC is not used for a few minutes, or the time it takes for an UPS (Uninterrupted Power Supply) to activate when there is a power outage.

Although you can change the settings using the graphical interface, the various settings are found in the most disparate paths.

With the command line, it's all within the same window.

Given the huge variety of settings that this utility performs, it also has a complex command line.

For example, you can get a report on the condition of a laptop battery.

By launching the *powercfg /batteryreport* command, a report is generated (in .html format) that can be consulted thorugh any browser installed on your PC.

Now let's see what happens when launching the command:

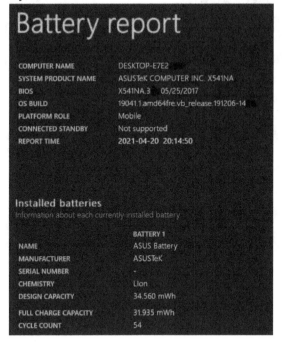

```
C:\>powercfg /batteryreport
Report durata batteria salvato nel percorso di file C:\battery-report.html

C:\>
```

After a few moments (depending on the performances of the PC), the prompt will show you (along with the relative path) that a report in .html format has been generated on the battery.

Battery report

COMPUTER NAME	DESKTOP-E7E2
SYSTEM PRODUCT NAME	ASUSTeK COMPUTER INC. X541NA
BIOS	X541NA.3 05/25/2017
OS BUILD	19041.1.amd64fre.vb_release.191206-14
PLATFORM ROLE	Mobile
CONNECTED STANDBY	Not supported
REPORT TIME	2021-04-20 20:14:50

Installed batteries

Information about each currently installed battery

	BATTERY 1
NAME	ASUS Battery
MANUFACTURER	ASUSTeK
SERIAL NUMBER	-
CHEMISTRY	LIon
DESIGN CAPACITY	34.560 mWh
FULL CHARGE CAPACITY	31.935 mWh
CYCLE COUNT	54

The report is very detailed and provides information on the battery health; for example the count of charge cycles.

Here is another example; a recently reinstalled laptop, which does not show charge cycles:

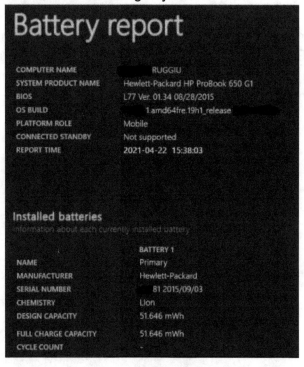

Battery report

COMPUTER NAME	RUGGIU
SYSTEM PRODUCT NAME	Hewlett-Packard HP ProBook 650 G1
BIOS	L77 Ver. 01.34 08/28/2015
OS BUILD	1.amd64fre.19h1_release
PLATFORM ROLE	Mobile
CONNECTED STANDBY	Not supported
REPORT TIME	2021-04-22 15:38:03

Installed batteries
information about each currently installed battery

	BATTERY 1
NAME	Primary
MANUFACTURER	Hewlett-Packard
SERIAL NUMBER	B1 2015/09/03
CHEMISTRY	Lion
DESIGN CAPACITY	51.646 mWh
FULL CHARGE CAPACITY	51.646 mWh
CYCLE COUNT	-

Below is the section of the file with the battery usage of tha Asus PC in the last 3 days:

Recent usage
Power states over the last 3 days

START TIME		STATE	SOURCE	CAPACITY REMAINING	
2021-04-17	20:17:00	Active	AC	98 %	31.687 mWh
	20:21:16	Suspended		98 %	31.924 mWh
2021-04-18	13:23:00	Active	AC	97 %	31.406 mWh
	17:46:04	Suspended		97 %	31.406 mWh
	22:38:42	Active	AC	97 %	31.546 mWh
	23:05:48	Suspended		98 %	31.665 mWh
2021-04-19	20:48:08	Active	AC	96 %	31.255 mWh
	22:45:52	Suspended		96 %	31.255 mWh
2021-04-20	19:43:10	Active	AC	96 %	31.050 mWh
	20:14:47	Report generated	AC	97 %	31.525 mWh

Below, the HP PC:

Recent usage
Power states over the last 3 days

START TIME		STATE	SOURCE	CAPACITY REMAINING	
2021-04-19	15:42:00	Active	AC	98 %	50.814 mWh
	16:59:06	Suspended		98 %	50.814 mWh
2021-04-20	08:37:06	Active	AC	98 %	50.425 mWh
	17:24:24	Suspended		98 %	50.425 mWh
2021-04-21	08:47:59	Active	AC	97 %	50.317 mWh
	16:50:55	Suspended		97 %	50.382 mWh
	17:09:52	Active	AC	98 %	50.382 mWh
	17:11:19	Suspended		98 %	50.382 mWh
2021-04-22	05:43:06	Active	AC	97 %	50.134 mWh
	15:38:03	Report generated	AC	97 %	50.231 mWh

On this page, you can observe the slow (and normal) battery decay of the Asus laptop examined:

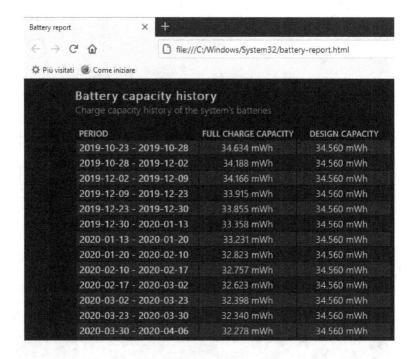

Looking at the first line, as of October 23, 2019 the fully charged battery capacity was 34.634mWh.
The charge capacity gradually decreases; on April 6, 2020 it had decreased to 32.278 mWh.

Another report is generated by the *powercfg /SYSTEMSLEEPDIAGNOSTICS* command, which allows you to check if the user of the PC has been away from the computer for some time and the PC has not been suspended when it was hoped for:

User Not Present Session 1

	TIME USER WENT IDLE	IDLE DURATION	SLEEP STATE ENTERED
1	2021-04-17 20:21:05	17:00:45	Sleeping3

Getting system information

The command that I'll show you now, performs a quick query on the system.
The utility I'm talking about is *systeminfo*:

```
C:\Windows>systeminfo

Nome host:                        DESKTOP-
Nome SO:                          Microsoft Windows 10 Home
Versione SO:                      10.0.19043 N/D build 19043
Produttore SO:                    Microsoft Corporation
Configurazione SO:                Workstation autonoma
Tipo build SO:                    Multiprocessor Free
Proprietario registrato:          Utente Windows
Organizzazione registrata:
Numero di serie:
Data di installazione originale:  22/11/2020, 02:37:07
Tempo di avvio sistema:           28/07/2021, 18:16:32
Produttore sistema:               ASUSTeK COMPUTER INC.
Modello sistema:                  X54
Tipo sistema:                     x64-based PC
Processore:                       1 processore(i) installati.
                                  [01]: Intel64 Family    1 92 S
```

This utility doesn't provide detailed information such as *"msinfo32"*, however it has a very useful feature; it offers a detailed list of the updates installed on the computer.

Below is a detail of the command output:

```
Amministratore: Prompt dei comandi                                    –  □  ×
Aggiornamenti rapidi:                    11 Aggiornamenti rapidi installat
i.
                            [01]: KB5003
                            [02]: KB4577
                            [03]: KB4577
                            [04]: KB4580
                            [05]: KB4586
                            [06]: KB4589
                            [07]: KB4593
                            [08]: KB4598
                            [09]: KB5000
                            [10]: KB5004
                            [11]: KB5003
```

The following list describes the purpose of each command:

/S system   Specifies the remote system to connect to.

/U   [domain\]user   Specifies the user context in which to run the command.

/P   [password]   Specifies the password for the given user context. If omitted, is prompted.

/FO   format   Specifies the format in which the output will be displayed.
                    Valid values: "TABLE", "LIST", "CSV".

/NH   Specifies to exlude the column header
                 from the output.
                 Valid only for formats "TABLE" and
                 "CSV".

/?   Display this help message.

Examples:
    SYSTEMINFO
    SYSTEMINFO /?
    SYSTEMINFO /S system
    SYSTEMINFO /S system /U user
    SYSTEMINFO /S system /U domain\user /P
    Password /FO TABLE
    SYSTEMINFO /S system /FO LIST
    SYSTEMINFO /S system /FO CSV /NH

Disk drive management and configuration

To manage and configure the disk drive without using the graphical interface, you can use the *diskpart* utility.
To access diskpart context, open a command prompt window, type diskpart and press enter as shown below:

Diskpart, allows you to operate on hard disks installed on a computer.
Not having a graphical interface available, you must first locate the list of the installed disks.

To view the list of disks, type *list disk* within diskpart context, as shown below:

Let's now check the output of the command:

N.disco indicates the disk number.

Stato   indicates the status of the disk (in this case online). If you were to view a disk offline, you can change its status by typing *select disk 5* and then *online*.
(in this example I indicated disk 5, but you'll have to enter the corresponding disk number).

Dimensioni   indicates the capacity of the HDD.

Disponibile indicates the space available for partitioning (not to be confused with free space for storage).

Din if there is an asterisk in this column, it means that it's a dynamic disk. If, on ohter hand, the columns is empty as in this case, the system indicates that it's a basic disk.

GPT if in this column you see an asterisk (as in this example), it means that the partition is of type GPT (GUID Partition Table).

If, on the other hand, the column is empty, it's an *MBR* (Master Boot Record) partition, that is the old HDD partition management standard.

To view the list of volumes, type *list volume*:

```
Amministratore: Prompt dei comandi - diskpart                                 -  ☐  ×
DISKPART> list volume

  Volume ###  Let. Etichetta    Fs     Tipo        Dim.     Stato
Info
  ----------  ---  -----------   -----  ----------  -------  ---------
--------
  Volume 0    D                         DVD-ROM       0 b   Nessun su
  Volume 1    C    OS            NTFS   Partizione  444 Gb  Integro
Avvio
  Volume 2         SYSTEM        FAT32  Partizione  260 Mb  Integro
Sistema
  Volume 3                       NTFS   Partizione  535 Mb  Integro
Nascosto
  Volume 4                       NTFS   Partizione  481 Mb  Integro
Nascosto
  Volume 5         RECOVERY      NTFS   Partizione  805 Mb  Integro
Nascosto
```

as you can see in the example on the previous page, the list volume command displays all volumes, partitions and CD / DVD drives (although, however, the diskpart command doesn't manage the latter).

The *list partition* command indicates the list of partitions, but only on disks that have "active state".
To view the list of partitions, you need to indicate the disk whose partitions you want to see.
In this PC, there is only one disk (Disk 0) and therefore I selected the disk by typing the command select disk 0:

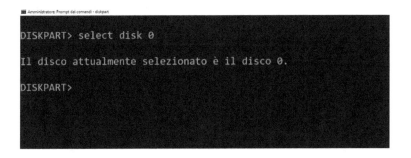

Now you can see the list of partitions

on the disk.

```
Amministratore: Prompt dei comandi - diskpart                                    —  □  ×

DISKPART> select disk 0

Il disco attualmente selezionato è il disco 0.

DISKPART> list partition

  Partizione ###  Tipo              Dim.     Offset
  --------------  ----------------  -------  -------
  Partizione 1    Riservato         128 Mb    17 Kb
  Partizione 2    Sistema           260 Mb   129 Mb
  Partizione 3    Primario          444 Gb   389 Mb
  Partizione 4    Ripristino        535 Mb   445 Gb
  Partizione 5    Ripristino        481 Mb   445 Gb
  Partizione 6    Ripristino        805 Mb   446 Gb

DISKPART>
```

In case you have connected an additional HDD, you can run the *rescan* command so that it's detected by the system.

```
DISKPART> rescan

Attendere. Analisi della configurazione corrente in corso...

DiskPart: analisi della configurazione completata.

DISKPART>
```

If the system does not detect the new HDD, it may not support hot swap, and in this case you will need to restart your PC.

List of Diskpart subcommands

Here is a list of useful commands, within "DISKPART" context:

ACTIVE   Indicates that the selected part is active; in this way, it signals to the BIOS and EFI that the partition is a valid system partition and that the system can use it for booting.

ADD   Create mirror of a simple volume. The disk must have enough free space, equal to or greater than that of the volume you want to "mirror".

ASSIGN   Assign a drive letter or mount point to the selected volume.
If no letter is indicated, the system will automatically assign the first available in alphabetical order.

ATTRIBUTES   View, modify or delete the attributes of a specific disk or volume.

CLEAN   Removes configuration information (partition and volume formatting).

CONVERT   Change partitioning from MBR to GPT and vice versa.

Ex. to change from MBR to GPT proceed as follows:

- Always back up any data on the disk if it has already been used.

- Access to **diskpart** context as indicated on the previous pages.

- type **list disk** and make a note of the number of the disk you need to convert.

- type **select disk** and the number of the disk you need to convert.

- type **clean**. (Running clean will delete any volume and/or partition on the disk).

- type **convert gpt**.

To convert to MBR, repeat the same steps, changing the last one as follows:

- type **convert mbr**.

CREATE   Create a volume, partition or virtual disk.

FORMAT   Format the partition or volume.

To exit the DISKPART context, type **exit** and press enter:

```
DISKPART> exit

Chiusura di DiskPart in corso...

C:\Windows>
```

For more commands, type **/?** in the diskpart context.

Defrag utility

Remember when years ago it was a good habit to periodically launch defragmentation?
Since the hard disk is written in random order, the file is divided into various segments and subsequent reading involves more work on the hard disk head (in the case of a mechanical HDD); all this wastes you time and at the same time impacts system performance.
By running defragmentation, the files are rewritten in an orderly manner, avoiding leaving empty spaces on the disk and making access to files faster (in particular with the use of mechanical disks).
Althouth today's SSD disks are much faster at retrieving files than mechanical disks, the option to defragment the disk has been retained.

This utility, uses the following syntax:

defrag <volume> [/A] [/B] [/D] [/G] [/K] [/L] [/O] [/T] [/U] [/V] [/X]

The wording "volume" indicated above refers to the letter of the drive that you want to defragment.

The following list describes each of the options for this command:

/A | /Analyze   Run the analysis.

/B | /BootOptimize   Performs startup optimization to increase startup performance.

/D | /Defrag   Performs traditional defragmentation (default). In a tiered volume a livelli, however, traditional defragmentation is performed only in the capacity tier.

/G | /TierOptimize   On tiered volumes, optimize files to reside in the appropriate storage tier.

/K | /SlabConsolidate On volumes with thin provisioning, perform memory allocation consolidation to increase the efficiency of memory allocation use.

/L | /Retrim On volumes with thin provisioning, it performs re-optimization to free memory allocations. On SSDs, perform re-optimization to improve write performance.

/O | /Optimize Performs the appropriate optimization for each type of media.

/T | /TrackProgress   IT tracks the status of a running operation for a given volume.

An instance can only show status for a single volume.

To see the progress of another volume, start another instance.

/U | /PrintProgress   Print the status of the operation on the screen.

/V | /Verbose   Print detailed output containing fragmentation statistics.

/X | /FreespaceConsolidate   Performs free space consolidation, moves free space towards the end of the volume (even on thin provisioning volumes).

On tiered volumes, consolidation is performed on the capacity level only.

Below are the methods of execution:

/H | /NormalPriority Performs the operation with normal priority (default: low priority).

/I | /MaxRuntime n   Only available with TierOptimize. Level optimization is performed for at least n seconds on each volume.

/LayoutFile <file path> Only available with BootOptimize. This file contains the list of files to be optimized. The default path is
%windir% \Prefetch\layout.ini.

/M | /MultiThread [n] Performs the operation on each volume in parallel in the background.

For **TierOptimize**, at most n threads to optimize storage tiers in parallel. The default value of n is 8. All other optimization ignore n.

/OnlyPreferred   When volumes are explicitly specified, defragmentation performs all specified operations on each specified volume.

This option allows defragmentation to perform only preferred operations, from the specified list of operations, on each specified volume.

Here are some examples of writing the command:

Defrag C: /U /V
Defrag C: D: /TierOptimize /MultiThread
Defrag C:\mountpoint /Analysis /U
Defrag /C /H /V

Viewing information about event logs

An utility that can be useful monitoring system event logs is *wevtutil*:

From Windows Vista onwards, this utility replaced those provided in previous Windows versions.
In fact, Windows Vista presented a large number of more complex logs, compared to previous versions which always contained the same "few and simple" logs.

Below is the list of commands for the wevtutil:

el (enum logs)   Typing C:\Windows>wevtutil el, you can view the complete list of logs on the system.

```
Amministratore: Prompt dei comandi
C:\Windows>wevtutil el
AMSI/Debug
AMSI/Operational
Analytic
Application
DirectShowFilterGraph
DirectShowPluginControl
Els_Hyphenation/Analytic
EndpointMapper
FirstUXPerf-Analytic
ForwardedEvents
HardwareEvents
IHM_DebugChannel
Intel-GFX-Info/Application
Intel-GFX-Info/System
```

gl (get-log) *logname*   It allows you to get information about a specific log.
For the smooth run of the gl command, you must also write the exact name of the log you want to check.
Help yourself with the el command to display the name of the log to check.

Below is an example with the WMPSetup log:

```
 Amministratore: Prompt dei comandi                                          -  🗗  ×
C:\Windows>wevtutil gl WMPSetup
name: WMPSetup
enabled: false
type: Analytic
owningPublisher: Microsoft-Windows-WMP-Setup_WM
isolation: Application
channelAccess: O:BAG:SYD:(A;;0x2;;;S-1-15-2-1)(A;;0x2;;;S-1-15-3-1024-31535
09613-960666767-3724611135-2725662640-12138253-543910227-1950414635-4190290
187)(A;;0xf0007;;;SY)(A;;0x7;;;BA)(A;;0x7;;;SO)(A;;0x3;;;IU)(A;;0x3;;;SU)(A
;;0x3;;;S-1-5-3)(A;;0x3;;;S-1-5-33)(A;;0x1;;;S-1-5-32-573)
logging:
  logFileName: %SystemRoot%\System32\Winevt\Logs\WMPSetup.etl
  retention: true
  autoBackup: false
  maxSize: 1052672
publishing:
  fileMax: 1

C:\Windows>
```

sl (set-log) *logname*   With this command, you can change the configuration of a log file.

ep (enum-publishers)   Enumerate event authors.

gp (get-publisher) Retrieve configuration information for authors.

im (install-manifest) Install event authors and logs from the manifest.

91

um (uninstall-manifest) Uninstall event authors and logs from the system.

qe (query-events) Retrieve events from a log or log file.

gli (get-log-info) Retrieve registry status info.

epl (export-log) Export a log.

al (archive-log) Archive an exported log.

cl (clear-log) Delete a log.

Chkntfs command

I recommend that you always run the chkdsk command on volumes that have not been shut down properly (either by human error or by power outage).

However, there are situations where running the chkdsk command is not possible or practical, either because it may take hours or even days to check thousands of files on the disk, or because the check may stop and keep hang.

You can use the **chkntfs** utility, to disable the automatic execution of chkdsk on certain volumes in the event of an automatic reboot of Windows due to an incorrect shutdown.

In practice, this utility allows you to manage the disk check (ex. automatic startup disabled of chkdsk) during the boot phase, so you can postpone the check disk guaranteeing you full control of the drive.

If you don't want "disk C" to be automatically checked at startup in the event of a bad shutdown, type as follows:

chkntfs /X C:

Below is the list of options available fot the command:

/D   Restore your computer to default settings; all drives are checked during boot and chkdsk is run on the bad ones.

/T:Time   Indicates the countdown before AUTOCHK starts in seconds. If the duration is not specified, shows the current setting.

/X   Excludes a drive from default check during boot. Excluded units are not accumulated between command invocations.

/C   Schedule check of a drive during boot; chkdsk will be run if the drive is damaged.

Fsutil utility (File System Utility)

The Fsutil utility (with the dirty option) is another utility that can be used to determine if the volume's dirty bit is set on the volume.

Automatically checks the volume for any errors by launching the AutoChk utility at next reboot.

To use the fsutil command, you must be logged in as administrator.

Below is the output of the fsutil dirty query C command:

```
Selezione Amministratore: Prompt dei comandi                    —  □  ×
C:\WINDOWS\system32>fsutil dirty query C:
Il volume C: non è danneggiato

C:\WINDOWS\system32>
```

Below is the list of supported commands:

8dot3name	File Name Management 8.3
behavior	Check the behaviour of the file system
dax	DAX volume management
dirty	Volume dirty bit management
file	File specific commands

fsInfo	File system information
hardlink	Real link management
objectID	Object ID management
quota	Quota management
repair	Automatic repair management
reparsePoint	Reparse point management
storageReserve	Storage reserve management
resource	Transaction resource manager administration
sparse	Sparse file checker
tiering	Storage tiering property management
transaction	Transaction management
usn	USN management
volume	Volume management
wim	Trasparent WIM hosting management

MRT utility

To detect and remove malicious software, you can use the MRT (Malicious software removal tool) utility provided by Microsoft.
After typing the command as below:

C:\Windows>MRT

You'll see the following window and by clicking on the next button, you'll start the procedure.

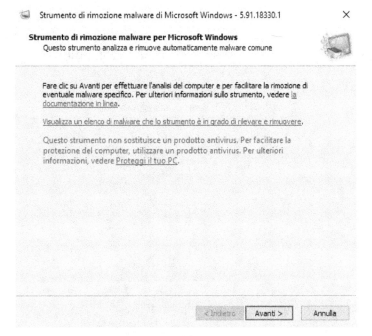

The screen will show you three options; I recommend that you carry out the complete analysis leaving the PC on at the end of the work/use day.
Although it can take several hours, it does a full and thorough scan of the entire system.
Select the type of analysis and click Next to start the scan.

Once the scan is complete, you'll see the result and simply click on finish to complete the procedure.

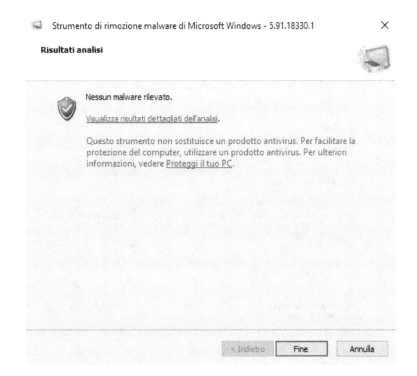

Strumento di rimozione malware di Microsoft Windows - 5.91.18330.1   ✕

Risultati analisi

Nessun malware rilevato.

Visualizza risultati dettagliati dell'analisi.

Questo strumento non sostituisce un prodotto antivirus. Per facilitare la protezione del computer, utilizzare un prodotto antivirus. Per ulteriori informazioni, vedere Proteggi il tuo PC.

< Indietro   Fine   Annulla

The MRT utility also has some options:

/Q o **/quiet** – mode without any graphical interface, forces the utility to run in silent mode.

/N   - detection only mode. If the utility finds viruses, it doesn't eliminate them.

/F   - requires a complete analysis of the system (it may take a few hours, but it's the most complete).

/F:Y   - as above, but in addition deletes infected files.

DispDiag utility

The *dispdiag* utility helps you to get some information on your display.
It generates a file that includes several information such as the video card model, the registry settings related to the video card and the operating system version.

Type the command as below and press enter:

```
Amministratore: Prompt dei comandi                                    -  □  ×
Microsoft Windows [Versione 10.0.19043.1110]
(c) Microsoft Corporation. Tutti i diritti sono riservati.

C:\WINDOWS\system32>dispdiag
```

The system will generate a file (.dat) indicating the path where you can find it:

```
Amministratore: Prompt dei comandi                                   -  □  ×
Microsoft Windows [Versione 10.0.19043.1110]
(c) Microsoft Corporation. Tutti i diritti sono riservati.

C:\WINDOWS\system32>dispdiag
Dump file: C:\WINDOWS\system32\DispDiag-20210728-233353-8236-6404.dat
```

Now check the file in the given path:

To read the content, you can click on the file with the right mouse button, select "Open with" and then choose notepad.

You'll see an output like the one below:

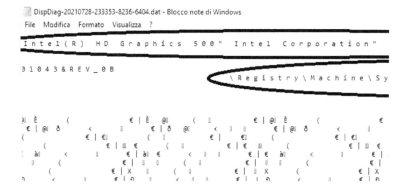

The dispdiag utility has various options to increase the details and quantity of information; you can view them by typing /?

.

Repairing system databases

Windows has several databases that are not often mentioned and they reside in the System Database Files (.SDB).
Not all SDB files are databases, some are simply text files.
Before using the command I'm about to show you, make sure that the file you're going to work on is actually a DB, opening it with a notepad.
The utility is **esentutl** (Extensible Storage Engine Technology Utility).

IMPORTANT: The esentutl utility is very powerful. Before editing any file, make a backup copy so you can replace it in case of error.
Using this utility incorrectly on the wrong file could cause the operating system to fail to boot.
To do some tests, I recommend that you get a test PC.

After this necessary premise, I will show you (to give you an example) the steps to follow to repair the policies, restoring local policies to default state.

Start a search on your HDD to check the path of the "secedit.sdb" file as in the example below and press enter:

Next, run Command Prompt as administrator and type the command given below:

esentutl /p C:\Windows\security\database\secedit.sdb

Despite being a very powerful tool, unfortunately you won't find much information about esentutl around... except in the Microsoft Knowledge Base.

In the example mentioned earlier, I showed you the /p option of the (Repair) command.

Below is the list of available options:

Defragmentation: /d <database name> [options]
Recovery: /r <logfile base name> [options]
Integrity: /g <database name> [options]
Checksum: /k <file name> [options]
Repair: /p <database name> [options]
File Dump: /m[mode-modifier] <filename>
Copy File: /y <source file> [options]

Checking the drivers

The utility *verifier* is used to verify that drivers are "trusted".

All manufacturers use this tool, in order to prevent drivers from making the system unstable due to their malfunction.

You should use this command (in case of malfunctions) to check that all drivers are genuine and have not been corrupted / modified by viruses.

IMPORTANT: Be very careful before starting a test of this type. It requires a restart of the PC and you may not be able to log in to Windows; you may be forced to log in in safe mode.

If you have the possibility, try it on a test PC in order to familiarize yourself with this utility.

In any case, before trying it, <u>make sure you have a backup of your data and know what you are doing.</u>

Typing the verifier command and pressing enter on the keyboard,

you'll see the graphical interface below;

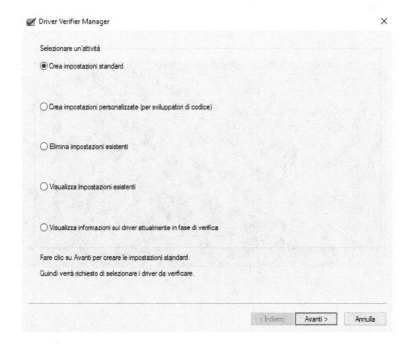

after selecting the first option "Create standard settings" on top of the list as in the figure, click on next.

if you have no idea which drivers are experiencing issues on your pc, you could select the first option at the top "Automatically select unsigned drivers".

However, I do not recommend this option because it could take a long time.

Select the last option in the list "Select driver names from a list" as shown below, to view a list of drivers to be selected on the next screen and click on next:

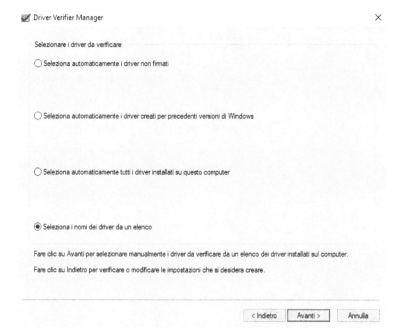

Scroll down the list and select the drivers you want to
check and when done, click on finish:

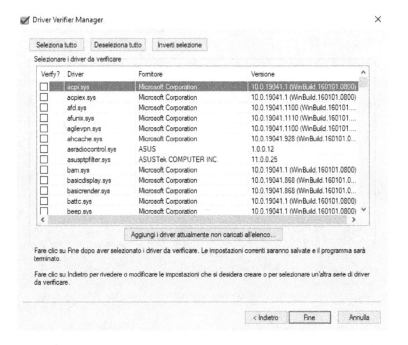

111

A pop-up will notify you that a reboot is required for changes to take effect.

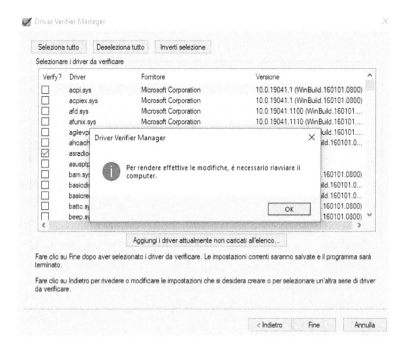

Regarding the command line, the utility verifier uses the
following syntax:

verifier {/? | /help}
verifier /standard /all
verifier /standard /driver <name> [<name> ...]
verifier {/ruleclasses | /rc} <options> [<ruleclass_1>
<ruleclass_2> ...] /all
verifier /flags <options> [<options> ...] /all
verifier /flags <options> [<options> ...] /driver <name>
[<name> ...]
verifier /rules {query | reset | default <id> | disable
<id>}
verifier /query
verifier /querysettings
verifier /bootmode {persistent | resetonbootfail |
oneboot | resetonunusualshutdown}
verifier /persistthroughupgrade
verifier /reset

verifier /faults [probability [pool_tags [applications [delay_minutes]]]]

verifier /faultssystematic [<options> ...]

verifier /log <file_name> [/interval <seconds>]

verifier /volatile /flags <options> [<options> ...]

verifier /volatile /adddriver <name> [<name> ...]

verifier /volatile /removedriver <name> [<name> ...]

verifier /volatile /faults [probability [pool_tags [applications [delay_minutes]]]]

verifier /domain {wdm | ndis | ks | audio} [rules.all | rules.default]

/driver ... [/logging | /livedump]

verifier /logging

verifier /livedump

Below is the list of options for the verifier command:

/? o /help
Displays this help message.

/standard
Specifies standard flags of Verifier Driver.

/all
Specifies that all installed drivers will be checked at next reboot.

/driver <name> [<name> ...]
Specifies that one or more drivers (image names) will be tested.
Wildcard characters (such as n*.sys) are not supported.

/driver.exclude <name> [<name> ...]
Specifies one or more drivers (image names) that will be excluded from testing. This parameter is applicable only if all drivers are selected for testing. Wildcard characters (such as n*.sys) are not supported.

/flags <options> [<options> ...]
Specifies on or more options that must be enabled for verification.
The flags are applied to all drivers that are checked by Driver Verifier.
The option values provided must be in decimal, hexadecimal format (prefix "0x"), octal (prefix "0o") or binary (prefix "0b").

Standard flag:
Standard Driver Verifier options can be specified with '/standard'.
Verification WDF is included in /standard but not included here.

0x00000001 (bit 0) – Special Pool
0x00000002 (bit 1) – Force IRQL Checking
0x00000008 (bit 3) – Monitoring Pool
0x00000010 (bit 4) – I/O Verification
0x00000020 (bit 5) – Deadlock Detection
0x00000080 (bit 7) – DMA Verification
0x00000100 (bit 8) – Security Checks
0x00000800 (bit 11) – Other Checks
0x00020000 (bit 17) – DDI Compliance Check

/query
   View Driver Verifier runtime settings and statistics.

/querysettings
   Displays a summary of the options and drivers
   currently enabled or the options or drivers that will
   be checked after the next reboot. The view doesn't
   include drivers and options added using /volatile.

/bootmode
   Specifies how Driver Verifier starts up. This option
   requires a reboot.

   persistent   Ensures Driver Verifier settings are
   persistent between reboots. This is the default
   value.

   resetonbootfail   Disable subsequent Driver Verifier
   reboots if the system is not restarted.

   Resetonunusualshutdown   Driver Verifier persists until
   an unusual shutdown occurs. You can use the
   abbreviation 'rous'.

   oneboot   Enable Driver Verifier for next boot only.

/persistthroughupgrade

Makes Driver Verifier settings persistent through updating. Driver Verifier will be activated during the system update.

/reset

Clears driver settings and Driver Verifier flags. This option requires a system reboot.

By the same author:

- Stupidario tecnico: 101 frasi dette dai clienti all'Help Desk (Italian Edition)

- Come cercare e ottenere un lavoro: manuale per il successo (Italian Edition)

  How to look for and get a job: manual for success (English Edition)

- How to buy high fidelity: bring quality audio into your home (English Edition)

- The ultimate guide for speeding up your pc: go faster! Expert tips for top performances pc (English Edition)

- Windows 10 al Top!: Trucchi e strumenti per sbloccare il potenziale del tuo pc Windows (Italian Edition)

- Windows 10 da riga di comando: Guida rapida alla command-line di Windows 10 (Italian Edition)

  Windows 10 at the command-line: Quick reference guide to Windows 10's command-line (English Edition)

- Windows 10 da riga di comando Part II: Guida rapida alla command-line di Windows 10 (Italian Edition)

Riccardo would love to hear about your experiences with this book (the good, the bad, and the ugly).
You can write to him at:
windows10atthecommandline@gmail.com